BOOM AND SLUMP IN INTER-WAR AMERICA

Tony D. Triggs

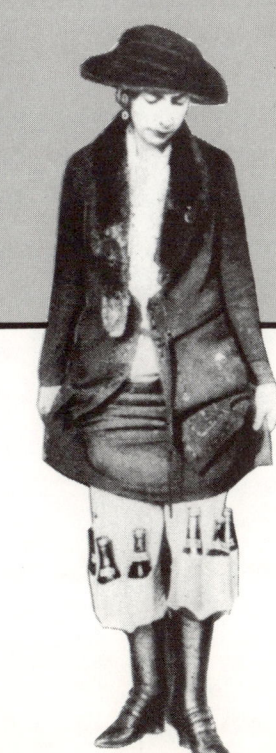

MACMILLAN

First published 1987
Reprinted 1987, 1988

Published by
MACMILLAN EDUCATION LTD
Houndmills, Basingstoke, Hampshire RG21 2XS
and London
Companies and representatives
throughout the world

Printed in Hong Kong

British Library Cataloguing in Publication Data
Triggs, Tony D.
Boom and slump in inter-war America—
(History in depth)
1. United States—Economic conditions—
1918-1945
I. Title   II. Series
330.973′091   HC106.3
ISBN 0-333-42318-6

Cover illustration 'The Builder' by G. A. Beneker,
by courtesy of Peter Newark's Western Americana

CONTENTS

Acknowledgements

The author and publishers wish to thank the following who have kindly given permission for the use of copyright material:

Elaine Greene Ltd on behalf of Studs Terkel for extracts from *Hard Times* copyright © 1970 by Studs Terkel; Harper & Row Publishers Inc. for extracts from *Only Yesterday: An Informal History of the Nineteen-Twenties* by Frederick Lewis Allen, copyright © 1931 by Frederick Lewis Allen.

The author and publishers also wish to acknowledge, with thanks, the following photographic sources:

BBC Hulton Picture Library pp 18, 20; BBC Hulton Picture Library/Bettmann Archive pp 5, 7, 17 top right, 19, 34, 52, 53; *Chicago Tribune* p 31; Peter Newark's Western Americana pp 8 right, 9, 13, 17 top left, 22, 25, 37, 39 top, 44 top, 44 bottom; Popperfoto pp 15, 17 bottom, 50; Topham Picture Library pp 8 left, 10, 14, 24, 39 bottom, 43, 46, 54; UPI p 28.

The publishers have made every effort to trace the copyright holders, but if they have inadvertently overlooked any, they will be pleased to make the necessary arrangements at the first opportunity.

PREFACE

The study of history is exciting, whether in a good story well told, a mystery solved by the judicious unravelling of clues, or a study of the men, women and children whose fears and ambitions, successes and tragedies make up the collective memory of mankind.

This series aims to reveal this excitement to pupils through a set of topic books on important historical subjects from the Middle Ages to the present day. Each book contains four main elements: a narrative and descriptive text, lively and relevant illustrations, extracts of contemporary evidence, and questions for further thought and work. Involvement in these elements should provide an adventure which will bring the past to life in the imagination of the pupil.

Each book is also designed to develop the knowledge, skills and concepts so essential to a pupil's growth. It provides a wide, varying introduction to the evidence available on each topic. In handling this evidence, pupils will increase their understanding of basic historical concepts such as causation and change, as well as of more advanced ideas such as revolution and democracy. In addition, their use of basic study skills will be complemented by more sophisticated historical skills such as the detection of bias and the formulation of opinion.

The intended audience for the series is pupils of eleven to sixteen years: it is expected that the earlier topics will be introduced in the first three years of secondary school, while the nineteenth and twentieth century topics are directed towards first examinations.

1 THE ROARING TWENTIES

The spending spree begins

'A car in every garage and a chicken in every pot.' In the 1920s this slogan was used by American politicians who were proud of their country's new prosperity. The troubled and rather hungry days of World War I had come to an end in 1918. Helped by American money and supplies, and also by American troops from 1917 onwards, west European countries such as Britain and France had defeated the Germans. Now the American troops were back home and factories which had been making weapons could start to produce 'consumer goods'. (In post-war America this meant things like radios, refrigerators and motorcars.) The bad times were over, people thought. Americans had helped in the war effort; now they could start to enjoy themselves and buy what they wanted.

Jubilation as American soldiers return home from Europe at the end of World War I

The war had held up the manufacture of many new products. For example, radio had been invented at the turn of the century. By 1914, when the war began, it would have been possible to make and market radio sets and to start public broadcasting, but this was delayed. The widespread introduction of refrigerators was also delayed in a similar way. Of course, these inventions (and earlier ones such as electric lighting) could only be used by people whose homes were wired to the mains. In much of America people had to wait until after the war for this. In 1923, when Calvin Coolidge became the country's president, he took his oath of office at home by the light of an oil lamp. Electric power had still not reached his farmhouse in the state of Vermont.

As new merchandise became available the American public made up for lost time. They filled their homes with the latest gadgets, buying on credit rather than waiting until they could really afford what they wanted. Many people had well-paid jobs in the factories which made the new products; their jobs were secure for as long as the public buying spree lasted, and few of them worried about their debts.

Cars and hovels – an unjust society

Cars had been available before the war, and the millionth Ford appeared on America's roads while the war was in progress. However, the number of privately-owned cars rose sharply as the war drew to an end. By 1920 Americans owned a total of 7 000 000 cars. By 1930 the total had risen to nearly 25 000 000, while the American population stood at 123 000 000 (roughly five people to every car). Thus the slogan 'A car in every garage' reflected the fact that the average American family possessed a car. (In Britain there was only one car to every nine or ten families at this time.)

Car ownership brought a major change in people's lives. An American writer described it like this:

boulevards: avenues

> Any [American] willing to get up early enough can look out of [his] own windows and see a trail of thousands of workmen's automobiles scooting down the boulevards to their factory or new building destination. Even ten years ago this great mass of labour had to live just around the corner in a hovel next to the factory or hang on street cars at six o'clock in the morning in order to reach the building [site].
>
> New York Herald Tribune,
> 29 October 1929

The car manufacturers' success ensured the prosperity of other American industries too. For example, they were major buyers of American steel, and of glass, rubber and other commodities. The manufacture and use of cars also ensured that the fuel industries made

A traffic jam in a New York street in 1917. Most of the cars are Ford Model 'T's

a good profit. In general, American business was booming. The public was ready to buy new products, and credit made it almost as easy to buy a car as a radio set.

However, American life had its problems too. For example, there were serious divisions in society, some of which were based on wealth and class. The newspaper writer ignored the fact that many workers could not afford cars and still lived in hovels. As we shall see, there were also many farming families who did not share in the general prosperity.

30% of working people; 70% of wages

70% of working people; 30% of wages

Questions

1   Why did so many new products become available after World War I? (You may be able to think of two or three reasons for this.)

2   Look again at the extract from the *New York Herald Tribune*. The writer tries to ignore certain things but he also reveals a lot about himself and his attitudes. How does he do this?

3   Look at the diagram on this page and sum up the information it gives you in one or two sentences.

Above: *a view from Brooklyn Bridge, New York, after the war*

Right: *the view from Brooklyn Bridge in 1934*

4 Look at the photographs. Some people say that the changes show how Americans felt about themselves and their country during the 1920s. What do you think these people mean?

Cultural and racial divisions

The difference in people's financial situation was not the only factor which caused divisions in American society. There were also major differences in culture, race and background. All three of these differences separated the ten per cent of the population who were black from the rest who were white. The black people were descended from Africans whom white men had brought to America to work as slaves. Slavery had been abolished, but in general the status of black people was still extremely low in the 1920s. Like their ancestors, most worked on white-owned farms in the southern part of America; the photograph on page 25 shows how poor and downtrodden some of them were.

Immigrants arriving from Europe after World War I

Divisions within the white population were just as serious. One in three were immigrants or the children of immigrants; the rest were descended from immigrants too, although their families had come to America earlier. Most came from various countries in Europe, and they differed in language, religion and culture. It was easy enough to pick up English, but religious and cultural differences (such as those which divided Jews, Catholics and Protestants) were harder to cope with.

The Ku Klux Klan

In the late 1860s some white people in the southern states had banded together in a secret society. They had called themselves the Ku Klux Klan (from the Greek word *kuklos*, meaning circle), and had done their best to terrorise blacks who tried to take part in local politics. The Klan had become inactive by the end of the nineteenth century but it sprang up again around 1920, affecting both the southern and midwestern states. As before, its members were middle-class Protestant men. This time, however, the victims were white as well as black, for members felt that white immigration was now excessive. Protestants were the biggest religious group in America, and Klansmen felt that established Protestant families were the only true Americans. They feared intermarriage with other groups, such as those who were still arriving from Europe. They said this would turn America into a nation of 'mongrels' or 'crossbreeds', for the children born to such parents would be partly foreign. In this way, the native culture and stock would slowly die out.

The man who revived the Klan was a clergyman called William Simmons, but members gave him the title of Emperor. Simmons feared something even worse than 'mongrelisation'. According to him, immigrants with outlandish beliefs were

> slowly pushing the native-born white ... population into the centre
> of the country, there to be ... overwhelmed and smothered.

The Klan had a cleverly chosen name, for a circle is completely closed – outsiders cannot enter it. In spite of this, there were plenty of Protestant men who could join, and membership reached a peak of over a million in the mid-1920s. It cost ten dollars to join the Klan, so the organisers quickly grew rich. They also made a great deal of money by selling the robes and hoods which members wore during meetings. There was even a 'Kluxer's Knifty Knife – a real 100% knife for real 100% Americans'.

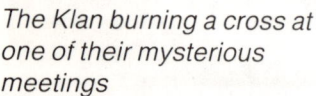

The Klan burning a cross at one of their mysterious meetings

Various things helped to make the members feel that they belonged to a secret society. For example, they had their own special way of speaking and writing: they began as many words as they could with the letter 'K', and they shortened phrases and sentences into secret words (such as 'sanbog', short for 'strangers are near, be on guard'.)

A Klansman's robe and hood were the most important things that set him apart from other people. They hid his true identity and gave him a weird, rather spooky appearance. The disguise (and the knives) helped Klansmen to terrorise other groups whom they hated and feared, such as Catholics, Jews, black people, drunkards and people who had been divorced. (In those days divorce was considered to be disgraceful.) Sometimes savage attacks were made; at other times wooden crosses were burned near people's homes as a warning that something worse was likely to happen soon. Often the Klan was successful in driving them out of the district.

Klansmen's crimes were rarely punished. Leading members bribed the police, and some important citizens were Klansmen themselves. In the end, however, the Klan's 'Imperial Kleagle' (or chief) was convicted of murder. This and other scandals led to the Klan's decline, although it lingers on to the present day in certain states.

Using the evidence: the aims and deeds of the Ku Klux Klan

Here are two contrasting views of the Klan.

A   In their Constitution Klansmen said their aims were:
  1   *to unite white male persons, native-born Gentile citizens of the United States of America, who owe no loyalty to any foreign nation, sect, ruler, person or people;*
  2   *to have as members only those who are totally respectable;*
  3   *to practise an honourable Klannishness towards each other;*
  4   *to shield the sanctity of the home and the purity of womanhood;*
  5   *to maintain forever white supremacy;*
  6   *to protect and maintain the rights and ideals of a pure Americanism.*

B   These are some of the things the Klan did:
  1   *They whipped a boy with branches until his back was in ribbons;*
  2   *they beat a negress and left her to die;*
  3   *they beat a white divorced girl into unconsciousness in her own home;*
  4   *they flogged a foreigner until his back was a pulp because he married an American woman;*
  5   *they lashed a negro until he sold his land to a white man for a fraction of its value.*

Adapted from an article by R. A. Patton
in *Current History*, 1920s

1 What sort of people did the Klan consider 'respectable'?
2 Make a large copy of the table below. Place a tick or a cross in each small box to show which groups could join the Klan and which were excluded. In the larger boxes write what Klansmen did to the groups they did not like. Use the information given in this chapter, especially passages **A** and **B**.

Black people		
White people		
Men		
Women		
Immigrants		
People born in America		
Gentiles		
Jews		
Roman Catholics		
Protestants		
'Respectable' people		
Divorced people		

Prohibition

The Ku Klux Klan resulted from self-righteousness, intolerance and fear of outsiders. The same things led to Prohibition (the banning of alcoholic drink throughout America). The campaign for a ban began before World War I, and was led by a group which called itself the Anti-Saloon League. (Saloon was the American word for bar.) People who wanted Prohibition blamed alcoholic drink for almost every social and family conflict. In doing this they exaggerated the part which alcohol played in these problems.

During World War I the Prohibitionists claimed that alcoholic drink was 'un-American, pro-German, crime-producing, food-wasting, youth-corrupting, home-wrecking and treasonable'. Nowadays some of these claims seem even more extreme than they did at the time; most of them also seem rather puzzling. However, we can understand the statement that drink was food-wasting if we remember that grain is a vital ingredient of beer and whisky.

Two things helped the 'drys' (or Prohibitionists) to get their own way. One was the sort of atmosphere created by war, which

This character sums up the artist's opinion of Prohibition

causes people to take almost any threat seriously, no matter how unlikely it may seem at first. Drink had been presented as a national threat, a sort of treason. Many Catholic families from Germany liked to get together and have a drink. Other Americans began to think that drink and disloyalty went together. They also imagined that workers who were dizzy with drink would not work quite so hard in the ammunition factories.

One other thing that helped the Prohibition campaign was the fact that most politicians wanted the Prohibitionists' votes, which could make the vital difference between election and failure.

During the war, Prohibition was gradually introduced in various states. It did not become Federal (National) law until 1920, two years after the war had ended. By this time many Americans were not sure they wanted Prohibition after all. As we have seen, they thought it was time to relax and spend their money more freely.

Bootleggers and gangsters

With its patchy support and many opponents, Prohibition could not be enforced. Some people's wish for drink was as strong as the Prohibitionists' hatred of it. Millions of people had valued the chance to go out and have a drink with their friends; and for many groups, such as European and Irish Catholics, drinking at home was a social custom. Now all the major breweries and distilleries had been shut down, along with the many street-corner saloons. However, drink could still be obtained. It was smuggled into the country by sea, or brought across the Canadian and Mexican borders. The smuggling of drink was sometimes called bootlegging. This was because in the early days of Prohibition the smugglers sometimes hid bottles of drink in the legs of their boots. Later, the 'bootleggers' often succeeded in smuggling drink by the crate or the wagon-load. These smuggled supplies were supplemented in various ways. For example, alcohol made in America for industrial purposes was often used illegally in the manufacture of whisky, gin and other strong drinks.

The illegal manufacture of drink was soon being practised secretly all over America. Some families simply made enough drink for their personal use; others ran small businesses, supplying their neighbours or the many 'speakeasies' (drinking dens) which had taken the place of the old saloons. In many cases people drank openly, for few Americans respected the Prohibition laws, and everyone knew what was going on.

In many cities, Prohibition gave gangsters the chance to become extremely rich. They brought in bulk supplies of drink by road and rail, and often they used false labels in order to trick officials.

13

There were 2 500 men with the job of enforcing the Prohibition laws throughout America. This was a tiny number when spread over such a large country. Moreover, the men were badly paid and could often be bribed to ignore what was happening. Police chiefs, too, were bribed and threatened to ensure that they ignored the gangsters' crimes.

Gangsters increased their wealth and power by racketeering. This involved subjecting people to threats and attacks until they agreed to pay the gangsters a regular sum to leave them alone.

America's most ruthless gangster was Al Capone (also known as 'Scarface' Capone). Based in Chicago, he and his men earned the following sums in a single year:

$60 000 000 from beer and liquor;
$10 000 000 from racketeering;
$25 000 000 from gambling dens and dog tracks;
$10 000 000 from dance halls and vice.

Al Capone fishing from his houseboat in Florida

Prohibition had been a disaster. The 'drys' had tried to force their ideas of good behaviour on other people, and this had given the

gangsters their chance. Al Capone once asked:

What's Al Capone done, then? He's supplied a demand. Some call it bootlegging. . . . I call it business. They say it violates the Prohibition laws. Who doesn't?

The St Valentine's Day Massacre

Gangsters used handguns or even machine guns to guard their shipments of bootleg drink, and to get rid of rivals. Shoot-outs occurred in city streets. In Chicago, the worst-affected city, gangsters murdered an average of 50 people a year throughout the 1920s. The most famous and bloody incident occurred on the morning of 14 February 1929. Five members of a bootleg gang were in their hideout with two other crooks when a car drew up outside the old building. Four strangers got out, two in policemen's uniform. They marched straight into the gangsters' den and riddled the seven men with bullets. When they left the building the two men

Victims of the St Valentine's Day Massacre

in ordinary clothes had their arms raised, as if they had just been arrested. This deceived onlookers who were wondering why guns had been fired. The uniforms had also deceived the dying victims. One man survived long enough to tell detectives about the incident. 'It was coppers,' the gangster said as he died. 'That's all I know. Coppers done it.'

In spite of this, suspicion fell on Capone and his gang. The dead gangsters' boss was a vicious thug called Bugs Moran, but even he was shocked by the way in which the men had been slaughtered. 'Only the Capone gang kills like that,' he told the police. Suspicion grew, for Capone's men had recently raided several drinking dens supplied by Moran. The massacre was simply the worst in a chain of nasty incidents.

There was now a national outcry against the level of crime and corruption in run-down cities such as Chicago. There were even calls for military action to break up the gangs and to restore law and order in the cities. Capone knew his men had committed the murders, and he feared that if they were brought to trial all sorts of new and unpleasant facts would be revealed. This would increase the danger of action against himself and all the gangs. One answer would be for the culprits to die. Sure enough, on the night of 27 February three of the men were drugged, then beaten and shot. Now the facts of the earlier killings would not be examined in open court; on the other hand, the latest killings brought fresh calls for action against Capone.

The trouble was that he did not seem to commit the most serious crimes himself. Moreover, he often made out that he was a peace-loving man: 'I want peace and I will live and let live,' he told a reporter. Most people found this hard to believe, but they could not deny that Capone gave massive sums of money to help needy people. At last, in 1931, Capone was imprisoned for not paying taxes. Two years later the Prohibition laws were repealed, and gangsterism began to decline.

Using the evidence: Prohibition and crime

1   Look at the cartoon on page 13. What do you think the artist feels about Prohibition? How can you tell?
2   Look at photographs A, B and C, then write down what you think is happening in each photograph.
3   How did bootlegging get its name, and which person in the photographs is copying the methods of the early bootleggers?
4   Both professional criminals and ordinary citizens tried to beat the Prohibition laws. Look at the photographs again and in each case say which sort of person you think is involved. Give reasons for your answers.

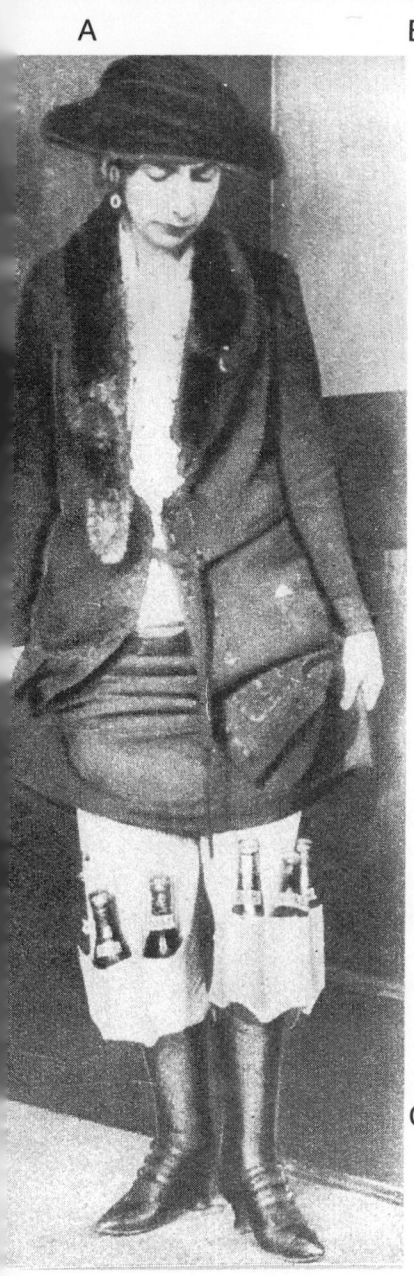

A

B

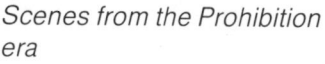

Scenes from the Prohibition era

C

DANGER AHEAD

Farming and poverty

As we have seen, America as a whole was very prosperous in the 1920s. People were buying cars, radios, refrigerators and all sorts of other goods. Most could afford alcoholic drink, although Prohibition had helped to make it scarcer and dearer. Many goods were rising in price, but wages were rising just as fast, especially in booming manufacturing industries.

Of course, people were not all equally fortunate. We know that by 1930 there was, on average, one car per family, but averages can often hide big variations. In fact some families had a number of cars, while others had neither a car nor a radio. The poorer families included many who worked on the land, especially in the southern states, where cotton had been a major crop. In the post-war period more and more clothes were made from synthetic fibres such as nylon and rayon. This had a big effect on fashion but it made life hard for those who depended on sales of cotton.

Other farmers had problems too. Many had borrowed money for tractors and other equipment, thinking that this would increase their production and hence their wealth. The trouble was that most were now producing more than they could sell. When they did sell their produce the price they got was insufficient to pay their debts and provide a good income. Over a fifth of American families were trying to make their living either from farming or farm labouring, yet the problems they faced remained unsolved. Some farmers went bankrupt and many farm employees were sacked. There was no question of people like these having one car per family. Men went hundreds of kilometres to the cities in search of work, and often their only means of travel was to leap onto trucks for a free ride.

Farming with new machinery

Even in the cities work was often hard to obtain. There were just enough jobs for those who were already living there, but few for the newcomers. Often they lived a homeless existence on the streets because the government failed to support those in need.

Mass production and unemployment

One thing that helped to limit the need for labour was the ever-increasing efficiency of the big corporations (companies). In the early years of the twentieth century, many small companies merged or were taken over by larger ones. Others were forced to close because they could not match the growing strength of their competitors. As a result, by the 1920s a few gigantic corporations were dominating American life.

Jobs were lost when the smaller companies ceased to exist. The big corporations used the newest and most efficient manufacturing methods, for they had the money to buy the new machinery which made this possible. With all their new equipment they could make things in enormous quantities. This was known as mass production. It meant that goods were very cheap, so plenty were bought and the factories made them faster than ever.

Mass production depended on each worker doing a single (usually boring) job. One man might have to work a handle to stamp out hundreds of pieces of metal. A conveyor belt would pass each piece to another man who would have a different job to do, such as punching or drilling holes in the pieces. A third man might have to bolt the pieces together in pairs. The employees could do more work by these 'production line' methods than would have been possible if each had had to change his tools repeatedly and do all three of the jobs in turn.

A British politician called Oswald Mosley went to the United States

Assembling cars by production line methods

in 1926 and he later wrote about what he saw in a factory where Ford cars were made:

> Each [man] performed some simple operation on the vehicle . . . as it reached him. . . . It was simplicity itself.
>
> The Ford factory produced the cheapest article and paid the highest wages in the world. In terms of money value, nothing on earth could compare with that original Tin Lizzie. Mass production for a large and assured home market is the . . . key [to success].
>
> Oswald Mosley: *My Life*, 1968

Tin Lizzie: the Ford Model 'T'

Manufacturing methods became more and more efficient during the 1920s. Because of this, the big corporations were able to cope with the growing demand for cars and other consumer goods without taking on extra workers. The number of unemployed Americans reached about 2 000 000 in 1928. For these people the new production methods meant years of despair.

In some manufacturing industries workers actually lost their jobs. For example, the textile and clothing industries shed many thousands of workers during the 1920s. Man-made fibres needed far less processing than cotton had done. Moreover, new materials meant up-to-the-minute factories, and these were highly automated.

In contrast, there was one industry where the need for workers was growing steadily. This was the motion-picture (or film) industry, centred on Hollywood. The first silent 'movies' were made and shown in America just before World War I. However, like other industries, it expanded enormously once the war had come to an end. Many of Chaplin's silent films were made in the early 1920s, and 'talkies' were introduced towards the end of the decade. Of course, mass production methods could not be used in filming, and thousands of well-paid jobs were created, especially in Hollywood.

A scene from Charlie Chaplin's film Modern Times. *Chaplin seems to be saying that working on production lines is unbearably boring. He finds ways of entertaining himself*

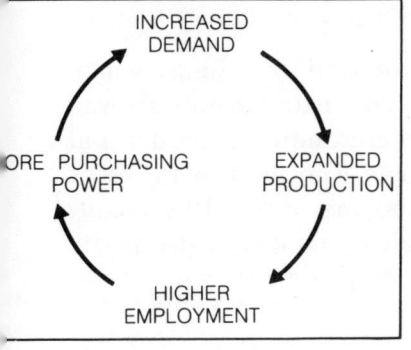

INCREASED DEMAND

EXPANDED PRODUCTION

HIGHER EMPLOYMENT

ORE PURCHASING POWER

A cycle of rising prosperity

Cinemas opened all over the country, and these too provided many jobs.

In general, America was a place of glamour and prosperity. Most people tried to ignore the recessions and unemployment in certain industries. However, the country's economy was not as sound as these people supposed.

Question

Look at the diagram on this page, which shows how America had slowly become more prosperous since World War I. What would you say was the weakest point or link in the cycle? Give reasons for your answer.

The big corporations: good or bad?

In some ways the corporations were beneficial; for example, they provided many jobs, although smaller companies might have employed a larger total number of people. Problems arose, however, from the corporations' excessive power and influence. The prices they charged and the wages they paid were often fair, but if they wanted to they could overcharge. This was easy for a corporation which had swallowed up all its competitors; it was also possible if two or three corporations agreed to fix a high price for a single product which all of them made. With no alternative source of supply, customers had to pay the high price. This was especially harmful if a corporation (or group) supplied parts or raw materials. By greed or inefficiency they could cause a slump in the industries which depended on them. It was bad enough if one corporation made workers redundant; worse still, it could cause unemployment throughout America.

At first it may seem surprising that the government failed to restrict the corporations' power. However, people with shares or senior jobs in the corporations often stood as candidates in national elections, or supported candidates whose views were similar to their own. In the end, many of those in government were on the side of the corporations, and they did not wish to curb their power or limit their profits.

There was one other thing which encouraged Americans to accept the independence and power of the big corporations: they knew that a pioneering spirit had helped to make their nation great. In the nineteenth century this spirit had been expressed by the bands of prairie farmers who had colonised the central plains of America. This phase in its history had taught the nation to value endeavour and enterprise. They did not like the law to impose too many restrictions, and the big corporations were able to take advantage of this.

21

The Florida Bubble

As we have seen, buying on credit was one of the things which helped American commerce to prosper, and many families owed money to banks or businesses. Farmers were finding it harder and harder to cope with their debts, but people who worked in towns and cities saw no need to worry. Heavy buying, assisted by credit, would keep the nation's factories busy. This would ensure prosperity and would protect the jobs of those in employment, who would therefore have no trouble in paying their credit instalments. This was the way many people thought. However, they were in for a shock, for a boom can sometimes lead to a slump, with widespread debt and poverty.

An example of this was 'the Florida boom' of the 1920s. Attracted by Florida's warm climate, many Americans started to buy houses along its shores. At first the buyers were wealthy folk. Many had made their fortunes as actors in Hollywood films; few of them needed to borrow in order to buy what they wanted. However, more and more people began to follow the stars' example. Some of them were attracted by the feeling that they were opening up a remote new territory. In a way this was true, for while some bought homes near beautiful beaches, most could only afford to buy houses (or building sites) in places that were rather wild and out-of-the-way. Even then, they had to pay by instalments, because they could not afford the full price all at once. In spite of this, the demand for land and houses increased, and prices rose sharply. Instead of putting people off, this actually encouraged them. Now they began to speculate by buying a house or a piece of land and selling it straight away at a profit. The new buyer might do the same himself. By the mid-1920s very few buyers actually wanted to live in Florida; often they never bothered to look at what they were buying, which might be part of an undrained swamp. Their only desire was to sell

Miami, Florida, in the mid-1920s

at a profit. They thought that they could make themselves rich by buying and selling repeatedly.

Some Americans did become rich by speculating in property, but in the end 'the Florida boom' went badly wrong. In 1926, sellers found there were fewer buyers than before. Perhaps by this time the genuine buyers had found themselves homes or had been driven away by the scramble for profits. At all events, many speculators were left with an unsold piece of land – and a debt to the person from whom they had bought it. They had paid a deposit, but how could they pay the remaining instalments? People let each other down, and banks, builders and private individuals quickly went bankrupt.

To make matters worse, two hurricanes tore through Florida in the summer of 1926. Some plots of land were already covered in rubble because bankrupt builders had not been able to finish their work. Now others were covered in rubble from homes which had been destroyed. 'The Florida boom' was certainly over, but people were still prepared to speculate, even if they had to borrow in order to do so, as we shall see in the following chapter.

Using the evidence: causes of the Florida boom

A writer called Lewis Allen, who lived in the United States in the 1920s, wrote a book about this period in American history. In the following passage, he gives us a detailed list of things which he felt had encouraged the Florida boom:

A   *... the climate – Florida's unanswerable argument.*

B   *The automobile, which was rapidly making America into a nation of nomads; teaching all manner of men and women to explore their country, and enabling even the small farmer, the summer-boarding-house keeper and the garage man to pack their families into flivvers and tour southward from auto-camp to auto-camp for a winter of sunny leisure.*

nomads: wanderers

flivvers: cheap cars

C   *The [confident spirit of] Coolidge Prosperity, which persuaded the four-thousand-dollar-a-year salesman that in some magical way he too might tomorrow be able to buy a fine house and all the good things of earth.*

D   *A ... revolt against the urbanisation and industrialisation of the country, the concentration upon work, the routine and smoke and congestion ... upon which Coolidge Prosperity was based. These things might bring the American businessman money, but to spend it he longed to escape from them – into the free sunshine of the remembered countryside, into the easy-going life and beauty of the European past, into some never-never land....*

23

real-estate: land

E   *And finally, another result of Coolidge Prosperity: . . . [the typical American] was fed on stories of bold business enterprise and sudden wealth until he was ready to believe that the craziest real-estate development might be the gold-mine which would [make him rich].*

Lewis Allen: *Only Yesterday*, 1931

An artist's comment on the rush to buy plots of land in Florida

INVESTOR—*Now, let's see, where did that agent say my lot was?*

1   a)   What do you think an 'auto-camp' was?
    b)   What is a 'never-never land'?
2   According to Lewis Allen, some people longed for 'the European past' and 'the remembered countryside'. Describe how these people's lives had changed.
3   Suggest one or two reasons why the demand for holiday homes increased in the 1920s.
4   Which word in paragraph C suggests that people were spurred on by envy? Why did they hope for good things 'tomorrow'?
5   What did people think they could do to make more money?
6   Look at the cartoon and explain what the artist was trying to say.
7   Look at paragraph A. What answer would *you* give?
8   According to Lewis Allen, how did the Coolidge Prosperity help to make people more reckless?
9   Someone has written, 'Each investor relied on finding a bigger fool. In the end they ran out of fools.' What do you think this statement means?
10   Why was this incident called 'the Florida bubble'?

3 | THE WALL STREET BOOM

The Coolidge Prosperity

Calvin Coolidge was President of the United States from 1923 until 1929. During this time the country boomed, with most Americans earning and owning more than anyone else in the world. People spoke of 'the Coolidge Prosperity' and they called their country 'America the Golden', 'the Land of Unlimited Possibilities'. They ignored the fact that unemployment was rising. They also ignored the very low wages paid to some workers.

Soon after becoming President, Coolidge said: 'The business of America is business.' He encouraged the American government to help big business as much as it could. The rich had their taxes reduced, because Coolidge thought that these people had the greatest influence on business success. If taxes were low they would have more reason to make a big profit, Coolidge thought, and the whole country would benefit.

The American government encouraged the growth of the big corporations because it felt that the advantages outweighed the risks. It raised the tariffs (or taxes) charged on foreign goods brought into the country. The main reason for doing this was that the government wanted to make people buy American goods, thus helping the corporations to thrive. However, things began to go wrong when foreign countries responded by raising the duties they charged on imports from America. So, while protecting their trade at home, the Americans had damaged their overseas markets.

Conditions in a shanty town

Perhaps it had also been a mistake to favour the rich. We have already seen that much of America's wealth belonged to just a few of its citizens. During Coolidge's time as President the wealthy people became richer still, while the wages of poorer people hardly rose at all. Price rises meant that fewer people could now afford the goods they wanted, even on credit. This in turn meant that corporations had falling sales at home as well as overseas. Some corporations tried to save money by sacking workers. Trade fell still further when this occurred, for unemployed workers were usually penniless.

Question
Look at the diagram on page 21, then draw a similar diagram to show what was going wrong by the late 1920s. The words at the top should be 'Less demand'. Decide the other words for yourself.

'Shares for everyone'

By 1928 it was clear to the bankers and other financial experts that 'the Coolidge Prosperity' had passed its peak. The country was now in a slow decline. In spite of this, the American public were still being 'fed on stories of bold business enterprise and sudden wealth'. Newspapers told of a pedlar who had spent his savings on shares in one of the big corporations, and had quickly grown rich as the shares rose in value. Stories like this were sometimes untrue or exaggerated. However, John J. Raskob, who was Vice-President of the General Motors Corporation, pointed out that anyone who had invested ten thousand dollars in his company in 1919 'now would be worth more than a million and a half dollars'.

In the past it was only the well-off who had purchased shares. Now ordinary American workers joined in a growing rush to buy as many shares as they could afford. Perhaps they could only buy a few, but a sharp rise in values could still make them rich. The stories of wise (or lucky) investments had made them forget what had happened in Florida. In the words of a writer called John Rublowsky:

stock: share

aviation: flying, aircraft

> *Almost any stock issue was gobbled up in the hope of striking it rich. Many of these ... were worthless. A Curtis Wright Aeronautical Company, for example, sold out an issue of 20,000,000 shares in early 1928 within weeks after it was put on the market. The company's principal asset, it later turned out, was an employee named Curtis Wright. The real aviation [company] was Curtis Wright Corporation, but aviation stocks of any kind were the glamour issue of the day, and speculators were quick to exploit this fact. The Seabord Airline, as another example, was actually a railroad and had nothing whatever to do with aviation. The name, however, attracted thousands of speculators.*

> J. Rublowsky: *After the Crash*, 1970

Election promises

Coolidge was due to leave office in 1929, and elections were held in the previous autumn to choose a successor. It some ways, 1928 was a bad time to have an election campaign. For example, it meant that politicians put off dealing with the weaknesses in America's economy. One of the candidates, Herbert Hoover, promised the voters that if he was elected he would give them 'four more years of prosperity'. His opponent, Al Smith, was forced into offering even more than Hoover had done. As a result, the country was swamped with slogans and boasts which encouraged an optimistic view of America's prospects. This increased the desire to buy shares.

Already, in March, nearly four million shares had changed hands in a single day. This was a record, but people predicted that sooner or later five million shares would be sold in a day. During the presidential campaign such days occurred frequently. Trading took place in the Stock Exchange building on Wall Street, New York. The scene there often resembled a street fight, with people scrambling to buy and sell at the best prices possible.

A Chicken for Every Pot

During eight years of rule we have built more homes, erected more skyscrapers, passed more laws to regulate and purify immigration, done more to increase production, expand export markets, and reduce industrial and human junk piles, than in any previous quarter century.

Prosperity is written on fuller wage packets, written in factory chimney smoke, written on walls of new constructions, written in bank books, written in business profit sheets, and written in the record value of shares.

Wages, dividends, progress and prosperity say, "Vote *for* Hoover"

A 1928 election leaflet (adapted)

Questions

1   What would you say were the weaknesses of Coolidge's financial policies?

2   Coolidge belonged to the political party called the Republicans. He made mistakes, but many voters had faith in his policies. We can tell this because they chose the Republican candidate, Herbert Hoover, to be the next president.
   a)   Name two or three groups in American society who were likely to have supported Coolidge's policies. In each case give a possible reason.
   b)   Name one or two groups who suffered under President Coolidge.

3   Look at the election leaflet on this page. Pretend you belong to the other main party (the Democrats) and write a reply of about the same length. You know enough to pick on several points in the leaflet.

Speculating in shares

In the past, people with shares in a company had usually held them for many years. They knew they could always sell the shares if they needed the money, and might get more than the shares had cost. However, as shareholders they received a modest annual payment (or 'dividend') from the company's profits, so they kept their shares for as long as they could.

Attitudes changed in the late 1920s. Now people started to buy shares in order to sell them again at a higher price, perhaps within a week or two. This form of speculation was not completely new, for the writer Mark Twain had given the following warning more than 30 years earlier:

October ... is one of the peculiarly dangerous months to speculate in stocks. The others are July, January, September, April, November, [June], May, March, December, August and February.

When Twain wrote this at the end of the nineteenth century the speculators were few in number and were mostly quite wealthy. Now, however, up to 25 million Americans were risking what little money they had. Some were desperate to 'get rich quick' because they were threatened with unemployment and poverty. Share prices rose as people competed to buy them before the price rose still further. They continued to rise until the sums invested were very much more than the companies were really worth. And they still went on rising, for no-one wanted to be left out, and sellers could take advantage of this.

People tried to buy their shares just before a sharp rise in value. This would happen if some good news about the company's profits or trading performance encouraged other people to buy. Speculators who heard the news at an early date would obtain their shares at the lower price. Then they would sell again quickly when they judged that the value had reached its peak. People could get rich overnight by doing this, so they listened out for clues about the future value of particular shares. Chauffeurs had a big advantage: they could listen to corporation bosses talking in the back of the car as they drove them to meetings!

Eager buyers in a broker's office

Questions
The photograph on page 28 was taken in 1929.

a)   Why do you think the people are queuing?
b)   Look at their faces. What do you think their feelings are?
c)   Do the people in the queue look rich or rather poor?
d)   What do you think the other men are writing on blackboards?

Risk and confidence

If necessary, people bought their shares 'on margin'. This involved obtaining a loan to cover the cost. They paid back the loan from the dividends which they received, or if they were lucky they might be able to pay it back after selling the shares at a staggering profit! In that case they would have money left over to trade in shares without any further need to borrow.

Buying on margin was risky because if the shares did badly the borrower might have to sell his house to pay back the loan. However, the chances of this seemed very small indeed. Writing in 1931, Lewis Allen listed some of the optimistic things which people had said:

I tell you, some of these prices will look ridiculously low in another year or two.

Just watch that stock – it's going to five hundred.

The possibilities of that company are unlimited.

If we all would only spend more freely, the smoke would belch from every factory chimney and dividends would mount.

People were not concerned if their shares fell slightly in value, since most falls were followed by rapid rises. One reason for this was that falls attracted bargain-hunters, who guessed that the price would soon recover. Their eager buying usually helped to bring this about. Thus people with shares that were falling in value rarely panicked; they simply waited for things to improve.

The key to the boom in shares was confidence. During the boom, which lasted from 1927 to the summer of 1929, this confidence sometimes seemed rather shaky, with big falls affecting a range of different shares at once, and some investors going broke. However, many investors bought at the new low prices and confidence quickly returned. As a result, the value of shares not only recovered but broke new records. The following extract explains how most Americans felt about purchasing shares:

It wasn't gambling; [it was] an investment in the glorious American future, an expression of faith in the endless, wondrous prosperity that blessed the land.

P. Sann: *The Lawless Decade*, 1958

Using the evidence: attitudes in the late 1920s

A modern author has written that 'In January of 1929 there was no-one to look over the edge of the cliff and note how far it was down to the bottom of the canyon'. The author seems to be saying that speculators on Wall Street were taking terrible risks, and that no-one realised how great the risks were.

We should not rely completely on a modern author. The following extracts show what people said and wrote in the late 1920s:

bull market: trading in shares with plenty of buyers, and prices therefore going up

A *[Shares] look dangerously high to me. This bull market has been going on for a long time, and although prices have slipped a bit recently they might easily slip a good deal more. Business is none too good. . . . I'd wait awhile and see what happens.*

A banker speaking in February 1928

B *A car in every garage and a chicken in every pot? No, TWO cars in every garage and TWO chickens in every pot.*

A politician campaigning in 1928

C *We in America today are nearer to the final triumph over poverty than ever before in the history of any land. The poor-house is vanishing from among us.*

Herbert Hoover, autumn 1928

D *No Congress ever assembled has met with a more pleasing prospect than that which appears at the present time. [In America] we have tranquillity and contentment . . . and the highest record of years of prosperity.*

Calvin Coolidge, autumn 1929

increment: profit

E *In my opinion the wealth of the country is bound to increase at a very rapid rate. . . . Anyone who believes that opportunities are now closed and that from now on the country will get worse instead of better is welcome to the opinion – and whatever increment it will bring. I think we have scarcely started. . . . I am firm in my belief that anyone not only can be rich but ought to be rich. . . . Prosperity is in the nature of an endless chain and we can break it only by refusing to see what it is.*

John J. Raskob: *Everyone Ought to be Rich*, 1929

F *Sooner or later a crash is coming and it may be terrific.*

Roger Babson, a financial expert, September 1929

G *Booms have always hitherto been followed by slumps but that was either outside America or else a long time ago. Post-war America is the country which never gets tired, never loses nerve and courage.*

From an article in *The Manchester Guardian*, 30 October 1929

H *Prosperity in decline? Why, man, we've scarcely started!*

An anonymous businessman, 1929

1   Copy out the following table, then put letters in each of the empty boxes to show which extracts agree with each statement. Be very careful when considering extract **G**.

America is great and glorious	
Prosperity will go on rising	
Beware! There are dangers	
Ignore fears and worries	

2   Which of the above statements sums up the four quotations in the middle of page 29?

3   Look again at extract **E**. Raskob was rather rude about people who disagreed with him. What effect could these people have? How could this come about?

A cartoon which appeared in an American newspaper during the 1920s

4   Look at the cartoon below. What does it say about attitudes to business before and after World War I?

Gambling fever – the road to ruin

As you studied the extracts you probably found that some people *did* foresee a disaster. In spite of their warnings, the wild speculation in shares gathered pace. Bankers tried raising interest rates. They hoped that this would cut down the number of shares that were bought with borrowed money, but 'margin' remained extremely popular. The trouble was that bankers did not dare to say or do too much about the dangers they saw, since this could ruin confidence and cause the very collapse they feared. While the bull market lasted, they and the corporation chiefs were enjoying huge profits, both as businessmen and as private investors. Like everyone else, they were 'hooked' on a sort of national gamble. In the summer of 1929 few people realised how near the end was.

THE WALL STREET CRASH

They roared like a lot of lions and tigers. They hollered and screamed, they clawed at one another's collars. It was like a bunch of crazy men. Every once in a while, when [shares in] Radio or Steel . . . [took] another tumble, you'd see some poor devil collapse and fall to the floor.

In Chapter 3 you read that the scene at the New York Stock Exchange resembled 'a street fight'. The description above was given at a slightly later date by someone who worked as a Stock Exchange guard. At first it seems that nothing had changed. However, during the Wall Street Boom people had scrambled to buy as many shares as they could, while prices rocketed. Now they were falling, and people were scrambling to sell their shares as quickly as possible. If you look at the graph you can see how prices changed direction, reaching a peak on 3 September 1929 and then falling rapidly.

This chart shows the price of important shares on three different dates

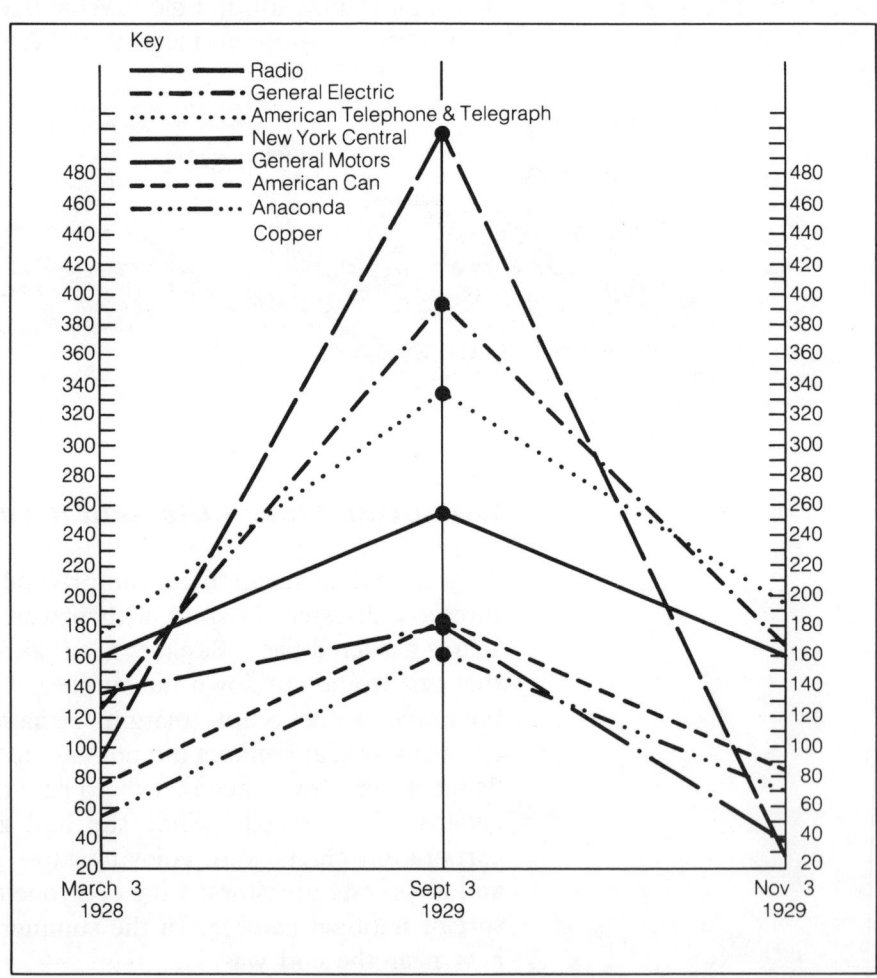

Weaknesses in trade and finance

Until September 1929, investors had simply ignored the fact that the corporations' profits were falling. As we have seen, one cause of this fall was that more and more people were out of work or earning low incomes. This resulted in lower demand, rising levels of un-employment – and further falls in public demand. Production had stayed quite high until the early summer of 1929. However, stocks of unsold goods were piling up in factory warehouses. By June or July, production had started a slow decline. This was one of the danger signs the investors ignored, for nobody wanted to end the fever of speculation.

Other things were going wrong too. For example, the prices of some raw materials such as copper, wool, wheat, sugar, coffee and cotton fell sharply during the summer months. The lower prices were a help to the corporations which bought these things for processing. However, they did enormous damage to the countries and corporations which produced them and sold them. The fall in prices occurred because stocks which had been building up for years due to overproduction were now allowed to flood the world's markets. These stocks had been held back in order to keep prices high for producers. However, they had grown enormous and no-one could see an end to the problem. When the stocks were released the fall in prices hit producers who had borrowed money from American banks and they found it hard to pay this money back.

Other foreign governments and organisations were also finding it hard to pay back loans received from American banks. Most of their problems were due to the higher import tariffs which had been imposed under President Coolidge. Like the producers of raw materials, they could no longer earn enough by exporting their goods to America.

International trade and money arrangements were unsound in other ways too. For example, during World War I the American government had loaned enormous sums of money to Britain and other allies in Europe. When the war ended, the defeated Germans were ordered to pay reparations (compensation) to the countries which had suffered most, such as Belgium and France. The French and Belgians used these regular sums of money to pay back war-loans received from Great Britain. Britain, in turn, used the money to pay her American debts. The trouble was that the payments required from Germany were more than the Germans could really afford, and during the 1920s they depended on loans from American banks.

Money was going round and round and bankers were powerless to deal with the problem. They knew that their foreign loans were unsafe, but they also knew that without the loans the whole cycle would fail.

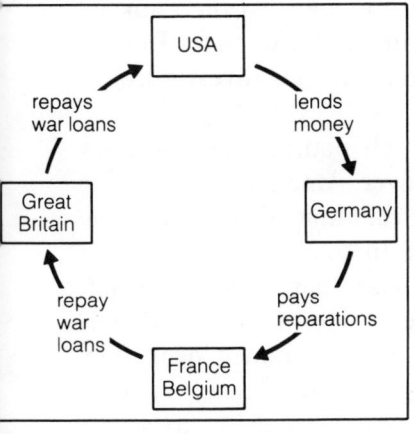

Money was going round and round...

Black Thursday – the panic begins

In September 1929 investors began to worry about the problems affecting international trade and finance. They also began to worry about the fall in production and profits at home. Some investors decided (rightly) that the values of shares had reached their peak. They felt that this was the time to sell while the going was good. Trouble began as more and more people hurried to put their shares on the market. Prices fell and the rush to sell became even faster. Conditions varied from day to day, but by mid-October the fall in prices was gathering pace.

At last, on 24 October (known as Black Thursday) investors panicked. At 10 a.m. the Wall Street gong was sounded as usual. This was the signal for trading to start. Almost at once it was clear that people were desperate to sell, for thousands of shares were being offered and buyers were very hard to find. Prices dived more steeply than ever, and sellers were forced to accept heavy losses. This was better than waiting and risking a further fall in prices; and some people *had* to sell because they were in debt already.

The ruin spreads

The news of what was happening on Wall Street quickly spread throughout America, for every town had at least one broker (a person who traded in shares on behalf of local clients). Each broker received the latest news from Wall Street by means of a 'ticker' or teleprinter, which recorded deals and prices on 'ticker tape'. The ticker tape showed that values were falling hour by hour. Brokers' offices filled with clients who wanted to check the latest figures; many investors found they were ruined, and 'some kicked over the tickers in a rage'.

The worst hit were those who had bought their shares with the help of a loan. The shares were a security on the loan and in many cases the shares were now worth less than the loan, so the bank or broker would want more money to make up the difference. Buying 'on margin' had not been a good idea after all – an investor could become homeless almost overnight.

Throughout Black Thursday orders to sell poured into the New York Stock Exchange from brokers all over America. This made the situation worse. It soon became clear that thousands who had bought on margin would not be able to pay their debts, even if they sold their shares and everything else that they possessed. The money had often been lent by brokers, who in turn had borrowed from banks. If brokers could not get the money back they would have no way of repaying the banks. In that case, some of the smaller banks would not be able to pay their debts to savers and also to larger banks to whom they owed money. This in turn could endanger some of the larger banks.

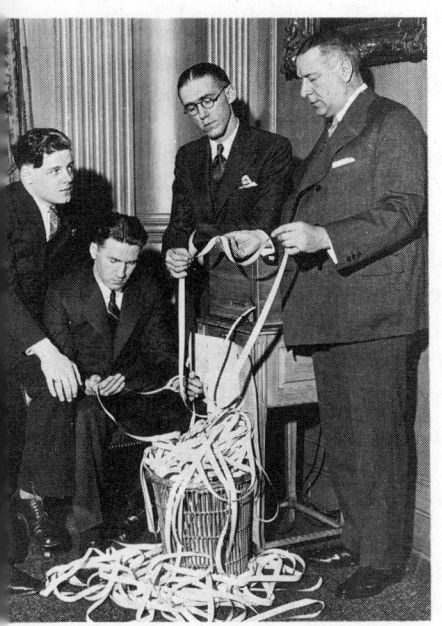

A broker and his staff receive news of falling prices

'Looking defeat in the face'

Until Black Thursday, the Stock Exchange was thought to be busy if over 5 000 000 shares changed hands in a single day. The sellers were usually making a profit; the buyers, too, would make a profit in their turn. On Black Thursday nearly 13 000 000 shares changed hands. However, people were selling at ruinous losses, and those who bought found values falling minute by minute. Besides the 13 000 000 shares which were actually traded, millions more were offered for sale without attracting a single buyer. 'Stock certificates that only yesterday had been the keys to wealth, power and position were [worthless] pieces of printed paper.'

On the floor of the Stock Exchange people scrambled throughout the day to sell their shares for what they could get. Others were in a state of shock; they were too dazed to act in a sensible way.

One saw men looking defeat in the face. One of them was slowly walking up and down, mechanically tearing a piece of paper into tiny and still tinier fragments. Another was grinning shamefacedly, as a small boy giggles at a funeral. Another was [begging] a clerk for the latest news of American and Foreign Power. And still another was sitting motionless, as if stunned, his eyes fixed blindly upon the moving figures on the screen, those innocent-looking figures that meant the smashing up of the hopes of years.

Lewis Allen: *Only Yesterday*, 1931

Desperate remedies

During Black Thursday a group of leading New York bankers did their best to calm things down. They sent an official to Wall Street to spend $240 000 000 on various shares. This must have been one of the most extravagant shopping expeditions in history. Despite the chaos, the official did his best to ensure that everyone else noticed what he was doing. He also wanted the press to report it the following day.

The plan was less successful than the group of bankers had hoped. Fewer shares were traded on the Friday and Saturday, but prices stayed extremely low. Bankers, brokers and politicians began to issue statements insisting that nothing was wrong. The trouble with this was that few people trusted the 'experts' now. Some investors were already penniless; as for the experts, they were clearly confused and worried like everyone else, having lost large sums of money themselves. They would naturally do their best to encourage investment and confidence, preferring to tell a comforting lie rather than face the unpleasant truth.

In the week before Black Thursday, when prices were already

drifting downwards, one man had written, 'I know of nothing fundamentally wrong with the stock market.' Others had predicted a 'merry comeback' – in other words, a return to quickly-rising prices. People had been misled – and ruined – by over-confident statements like these. They were not in a mood to be reassured when a leading banker said there had been just 'a little' urgent selling on Thursday. A little indeed! Nor were investors reassured when a stockbroker told them: 'The selling was panicky, brought on by hysteria.... Conditions are good.' As well as reporting statements such as these, the press carried stories of bankrupt people jumping from skyscrapers. News like this had more effect than soothing words.

Using the evidence: twisting the truth

The events of 1929 were largely due to the false or distorted ideas people had. This is how a modern author explains what occurred:

> *No one was responsible for the great Wall Street crash. No one [planned] the speculation which preceded it. Both were the product of the free choice and decision of hundreds of thousands of individuals. [They] were not led to the slaughter. They were [driven] to it by the ... lunacy which has always seized people who [think] that they can become very rich.*
> J. K. Galbraith: *The Great Crash*, 1961

We have already seen the truth of this. We have also seen that excitement, fear and rumours often went together. We can confirm this if we study the following press report which appeared on the day after Black Thursday:

> *Huge crowds ... surged up and down the narrow streets of the financial district ... in search of excitement.*
>   *Baseless rumours about the failure of [brokers], banks and large speculators were considered with bated breath and further excited the curious throng.... The appearance of newsboys with extras was the cue for more running and shouting.... [Additional] police were called out to handle the situation.*
>   *Persons bruised by the rough milling brought ambulances clanging into Wall Street, and more rumours were started about the collapse of traders on the floor of the Exchange. [There were] reports that six traders had been carried [out] on stretchers. The sudden illness of someone in a law office ... brought an ambulance down Broad Street and started rumours that a trader, caught [by the falling price of shares], had jumped from a window. From then on reports were frequent that brokers and others had jumped from windows.*
> *The New York Herald Tribune*, 25 October 1929

failure: bankruptcy

extras: extra editions

In your exercise book, copy the table shown below. Each empty box will contain a sentence, so make your table very large. You will still need to keep your answers brief; use your own words wherever you can.

	A	B	C
Truth			
Rumour			
False reports			

1   Look at the third paragraph of the passage, which shows how two different rumours developed. Beside the word 'Truth', in column **A** say what really happened to start the first rumour. Underneath, say what the rumour was. Finally, in the bottom space, describe the false report into which the rumour developed.
2   Use column **B** to show how the second rumour developed.
3   Look at the first two paragraphs, which describe a further rumour. Say what it was in the 'Rumour' space in column **C**. Then guess the sort of thing which might have started it off and write your idea in the upper space. Finally, use the lower space to say how it might have developed.
4   Compare the photograph on page 28 with the one on page 34. Do you think the brokers' mood is different? How can you tell?

Black Tuesday

Brokers worked throughout the weekend trying to bring their accounts up to date. They would soon have to contact many of their clients, who would hear bad news about their shares and debts on Monday or Tuesday. Some would then be forced to sell; others would sell before the values fell still further.

Everyone knew that the week would start very badly on Wall Street. Sure enough, on Monday 28 October nine million shares were traded, and thousands of millions of dollars were lost. In spite of this, no-one expected another day as bad as Black Thursday. They were in for a shock, however, for Tuesday 29 October was even worse. As soon as the gong had sounded there was a rush to sell. Shares which the bankers had bought a few days earlier were back on the market. This increased the general frenzy to sell at all costs.

There was so much trading that the teleprinters could not keep up with it. By lunchtime, the news reaching brokers throughout America was one and a half hours out of date. This fact added to people's fears. Normally, prices would not have changed much in

Anxious and inquisitive people flock into Wall Street as share prices plunge

37

such a short time, but things were different now. When news about particular shares came through by telephone it was always worse than people expected. It proved that the ticker tape was hopelessly wrong; it was so out-of-date as to be almost meaningless. As usual it showed just the final figure or two of each value. In normal times, investors could easily check the rest of the value.

Today, when they saw a run of symbols and figures like

R   WX

  6. 5½. 5. 4.   9. 8^{7311}_{8424}. 8. 7½. 7.

they could not be sure whether the price of '6' shown for Radio meant 66 or 56 or 46; whether Westinghouse was sliding from 189 to 187 or from 179 to 177.

Lewis Allen: Only Yesterday, 1931

'Panic raging overhead'

On Wall Street, the Governing Committee of the Stock Exchange held an urgent meeting. It was now early afternoon and frenzied selling had reached a new peak. Some members wanted to close the Exchange for the rest of the day. They thought this might reduce the panic that was seizing the nation; it would also enable brokers to study their accounts, and thus see which investors, brokers and banks had been ruined. This would make depressing news, but it had to be faced. Other committee members felt that the Exchange should stay open, as closure might increase the panic of people who still had shares to sell. It could also lead to trouble on the streets of New York. On Black Thursday, crowds of curious people had flocked into Wall Street. Many had 'wanted grandstand seats as their dreams of riches washed away in streams of ticker tape.' Few of the people had been unruly; even so, an unwise decision to close the Exchange could lead to chaos, or even to riots.

At the time of the meeting, Richard Whitney was Vice-President of the Stock Exchange. In the following passage he describes what the meeting was like:

The forty governors came in groups of two or three.... The office they met in was never designed for large meetings of this sort, with the result that most of the governors were compelled to stand, or to sit on tables. As the meeting progressed, panic was raging overhead on the floor.... The feeling of those present was revealed by the habit of continually lighting cigarettes, taking a puff or two, putting them out and lighting new ones....

From a speech made by Richard Whitney in 1930

In the end, the governors made up their minds to keep the Stock Exchange open until Thursday evening, then to close it until the following Monday. This was probably very wise. No-one could say that the Stock Exchange was closing in panic, but dealers would have all the time they needed to sort things out.

Questions

1   Why do you think the bankers made a show of buying shares on Black Thursday?

2   a)   What did the bankers do with their shares soon afterwards?
    b)   Why do you think they did this, and how did it have a bad effect?

3   a)   Pick out one or two clues which show that the Wall Street governors were trying to meet in secret.
    b)   Why do you think they wanted to do this?
    c)   What state were they in? How can you tell?

4   Look at the cartoon on this page. What do you think the artist was saying?

Reaching rock bottom

Trading was calm on the Wednesday and Thursday, and the Stock Exchange reopened calmly on the following Monday. There were no more days of frantic selling, and it sometimes looked as if prices would rise from the depths to which they had sunk on Black Tuesday. However, the general trend was still downwards, and throughout the first two weeks of November new record lows were repeatedly set for different shares. Finally, on 13 November, share values reached their lowest levels overall. After this they made a very slow and uncertain recovery; the process lasted years, not days. In any case, it was far too late to repair the damage which the Wall Street Crash had done to the country. America was rapidly sinking into a deep depression, with unemployment, despair and starvation taking the place of boom and prosperity.

The Stock Exchange – closed because of the crisis

THE GREAT DEPRESSION

We thought American business was [as solid as a rock]. We were the prosperous nation, and nothing could stop us now. A brown-stone house was forever. You gave it to your kids and they put marble fronts on it. There was a feeling of continuity. If you made it, it was there forever. Suddenly, the big dream exploded. The impact was unbelievable.

E. Y. Harburg, quoted in S. Terkel's book
Hard Times, 1970

These words describe the shock people felt as unemployment and poverty spread throughout America. In some ways it is hard to understand why the Wall Street Crash led to national depression. Up to September, millions of people had made themselves rich with stocks and shares. Some of these people were penniless now, but most were simply back where they started. Many businesses, too, had survived the Crash. A few banks (and quite a number of brokers) had gone out of business, but the big corporations were still intact. Some people said that a corporation's wealth was equal to the total value of the shares it had issued. Judged like this, the wealth of the major corporations had risen with the Wall Street Boom and slumped when the Wall Street Crash occurred, so they too were simply back where they started. In any case, the corporations' plant, patents and other assets had generally stayed fairly constant in value.

Business as usual

Experts could no longer claim that shares were perfectly sound. Even so, they could still insist that business was carrying on as normal. Companies paid for full-page advertisements telling the public:

Wall Street may sell stocks, but Main Street is still buying goods.

The ticker may slow down, but production is going right ahead.

According to the new President, Herbert Hoover:

The fundamental business of the country ... the production and distribution of goods, is on a sound and prosperous basis.

A leading banker called Eugene Stevens claimed:

There is nothing in the business situation to justify any nervousness.

And the millionaire J. D. Rockefeller said in a speech:

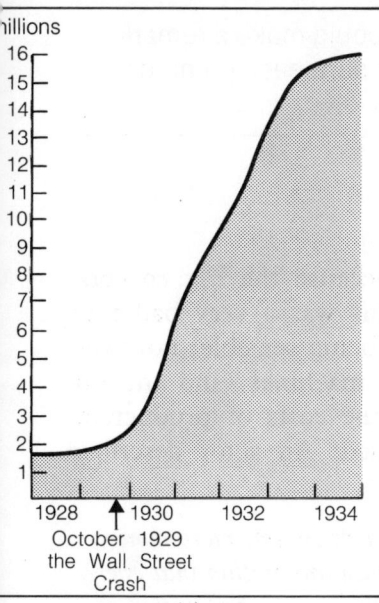

millions
```
16
15
14
13
12
11
10
 9
 8
 7
 6
 5
 4
 3
 2
 1
   1928    1930    1932    1934
        ↑
   October 1929
   the Wall Street
   Crash
```

Rising levels of unemployment

There is nothing in the business situation to warrant the destruction of [share] values that has taken place.

When he went on to say that he and his son had been buying shares for several days, someone asked bitterly, 'Who else has any money left?'

It was true that the number of unemployed people had risen because of business failures. By the end of 1929 it was approaching 2 500 000. It was also true that a smaller number had lost their savings and even their homes. Even so, about 90 per cent of American workers still had jobs. The real trouble came when the rise in unemployment gathered pace. This occurred because those who were ruined or thrown out of work in the Wall Street Crash had nothing to spend; fewer goods were bought in the shops so more workers lost their jobs. The cycle had already started by 1929, but after the Crash it went faster and faster – so fast that no-one was able to stop it. As a result, the Depression went from bad to worse, and within four years nearly a third of American adults were out of work. The graph shows how quickly the level of unemployment rose.

In the summer of 1929 the National Association of Merchant Tailors had tried to push up sales by saying that working men should have 20 suits, a dozen hats, eight overcoats and 24 pairs of shoes. Now there were millions of unemployed men who had one shabby suit and a single pair of battered shoes. As these wore out it became quite painful to tramp the streets in search of food or casual work.

Some people suffered terrible hardship, especially if they were unskilled or black. Racial prejudice against black people was still very strong. In the following passage a member of America's black community remembers his own experiences:

I said, 'I'm going out in the world to get me a job.' And God help me, I couldn't get anything.

I'd write, 'Dear Mother, I'm doin' wonderful and [I hope] you're all fine.' That was in Los Angeles and I was sleeping under some steps and there was some paper over me.

I wouldn't eat [for] two or three days. . . . I was too sick to eat. It's a wonder I didn't die.

I went to the hospital there in Los Angeles. They said, 'Where do you live?' . . . . Police says, 'OK, put him in jail.' I'd get ninety days for vag.

Louis Banks, quoted in S. Terkel's book
Hard Times, 1970

vag: vagrancy, being a tramp

Question
Look at the statements quoted on pages 40 and 41. Copy out three of them and in each case add a question or comment to challenge the statement. In one case you could add the words, 'So why did

everyone sell their shares?' In another you could make a remark about unemployment or unsold stock. Make sure each comment matches the statement.

'The greatest tragedy of all'

The Depression was made much worse because the big corporations (and wealthy individuals) felt that this was a very bad time for new investment. In one way they were being sensible; however, they were over-cautious, preferring to let machines (and the unemployed) stand idle rather than risking the costs of production. A very rich country was therefore paralysed. An actor described what this was like:

> *We got more wheat, more corn, more food, more cotton, more money in the banks, more everything in the world than any nation that ever lived ever had, yet we are starving to death. We are the first nation in the history of the world to go to the poorhouse in an automobile.*
>
> Will Rogers, November 1931

In the following passage a modern author describes the same problem:

> *Everything necessary for prosperity was available, the machinery as well as the know-how and [materials]. Never had America experienced such a contradiction. People were out of work, but the machines were idle. People needed clothes [and homes], but the factories and builders did nothing. People were starving, but crops had not been sown or were rotting unharvested in the fields.*
>
> *This was the greatest tragedy of all.... The depression was not caused by any natural failure. It was the failure of a system in which the [driving] force was ... profit. Business, [left alone] by government, had [failed] to satisfy the needs of the people.*
>
> J. Rublowsky: *After the Crash*, 1970

The final point this author makes is very important. We have already seen that Americans disliked government interference. They had always believed that people ought to be left alone to succeed (or fail) in whatever they did. This spirit of independence and enterprise is sometimes known as 'rugged individualism', although we have to remember that businesses, too, liked to 'go it alone'. Because of these feelings, governments had done very little during the 1920s to regulate what businessmen and investors did. After the Crash, some people tried to blame them for this. Hungry families began to ask for government help, and many people called for spending on dams, railways, and other projects to give people work. As we shall see, President Hoover resisted these demands, and he therefore became extremely unpopular.

Smile away the Depression!

Smile us into Prosperity!
wear a
SMILETTE!

This wonderful little gadget will
solve the problems of the Nation!

APPLY NOW AT YOUR CHAMBER OF COMMERCE
OR THE REPUBLICAN NATIONAL COMMITTEE

WARNING—*Do not risk Federal arrest by looking glum!*

Questions

1 Look at the leaflet on this page. What does it show?

2 Which political party might have issued these leaflets, and what point do you think they were trying to make?

3 Look at the warning on the bottom.
   a) What might President Hoover have said about these words?
   b) Why might Louis Banks have agreed with them?

4 a) Why did Banks write a cheerful letter home?
   b) Was he wanting to do what the leaflet said?
   c) Which groups of people treated him badly?

Hoovervilles

Poverty-stricken families who had lost their homes built shanty towns on pieces of waste ground:

> *[There were] people living in old, rusted-out car bodies [or] in shacks made of orange crates. One family with a whole lot of kids were living in a piano box. This wasn't just a little [district], this was maybe ten miles wide and ten miles long. People living in whatever they could junk together.*
>
> Peggy Terry, quoted in S. Terkel's book
> *Hard Times*, 1970

The shanty towns were often known as 'Hoovervilles'. This was a bitter or humorous way of making the shanty towns sound posh.

A Hooverville

Lining up for a cheap meal

Trying to make ends meet during the Depression

It was also a way of pinning the blame on President Hoover. Other similar phrases also came into use. People who slept under layers of newspaper said they were using 'Hoover blankets'. Men who kept their trouser pockets inside out to show they were penniless called their pockets 'Hoover flags'. (This practice gave them a sense of brotherhood, and it helped them when they begged for food.)

Shops would sometimes give these people 'figs that had spoiled and canned fruit that had gone a bit sour'. These could be taken 'home' to their families. The men themselves queued for hours to get some soup at a charity kitchen. Sometimes the rest of the family joined the queue as well.

While this was happening food was being destroyed in many parts of the country. In some areas 'wheat . . . was being poured into the ocean'. Elsewhere, producers would 'put up a rick of oranges and apples, put gasoline over it and set fire to them'. All this was being done to keep prices high, for only then could farmers afford to transport goods to market.

Hunger and shame

Despite the efforts of many parents, children went hungry. A headmaster told of a 12-year-old boy who fainted at school. '[It] was two o'clock in the afternoon. . . . He said he was hungry. He had not had anything to eat since the day before.'

Some parents stole for the sake of their children. A father explained, 'If I were honest it would be a sin . . . as it would deprive my children of food.' Even so, the need to steal was very upsetting. One man who said he had stolen coal went on to say, 'You may wonder how this has affected my mind.'

For some men and women, hunger and shame had come very suddenly. Like everyone else, they believed in 'rugged independence', but now they had failed to live up to this principle. Many could hardly bear to eat food which was given or stolen; accepting a bowl of soup made them feel worthless. One woman said, 'If I could only have just one meal that my husband had bought, the food would taste so much better.' However, not everyone felt like this.

> *I remember it was fun. It was fun going to the soup line. 'Cause we all went down the road, and we laughed and we played. The only thing we felt was that we were hungry and we were going to get food. Nobody made us feel shamed.*
>
> Peggy Terry, quoted in S. Terkel's book
> *Hard Times*, 1970

Using the evidence: conflicting attitudes

The following statements, made by prominent people during the great Depression, come from Susan Winslow's book, *Brother, Can You Spare a Dime?* published in 1975.

A *I see nothing in the present situation that is either menacing or warrants pessimism. During the winter months there may be some slackness or unemployment, but hardly more than at this season each year. I have every confidence that there will be a revival of activity in the Spring and that during the coming year the country will make steady progress.*

Andrew Mellon, Secretary of the Treasury, January 1930

B *We have been passing through one of those great economic storms which periodically bring hardship and suffering upon our people. I am convinced we have now passed the worst and with continued unity of effort we shall rapidly recover. There is one certainty in the future of a people [such as ourselves] – that is, prosperity.*

President Hoover, May 1930

C *We can say with satisfaction of this period of nearly twenty months of continuous economic [decline] that we have had fewer strikes and lockouts than in normal times; that we have had no mob violence worth noting . . . with only local and unnecessary exceptions there has been no starvation. . . .*

The first duty of the Government – that is, to secure social tranquillity and to maintain confidence in our institutions – has been performed.

President Hoover, May 1931

D *The average man won't really do a day's work unless he is caught and cannot get out of it. There is plenty of work to do, if people would do it.*

Henry Ford, millionaire car manufacturer, March 1931

E *There is not an unemployed man in the country that hasn't contributed to the wealth of every millionaire. . . . The working classes didn't bring this on, it was the big boys thought the [boom] was going to last forever, and overbought, overmerged and [overspent].*

Will Rogers, November 1931

The following quotations come from Studs Terkel's book *Hard Times*, published in 1970. They show how ordinary people remembered the Depression.

F *You'd get word somebody's gonna build a building. . . . So the next morning you get up at five o'clock and you dash over there. You got a big tip. There's three thousand men there, carpenters, cement men, guys who knew machinery and everything else. These fellas always had faith that the job was [real]. More and more men were after fewer and fewer jobs. So San Francisco just ground to a halt. Nothing was moving.*

Ed Paulsen

Will there be any jobs for these men?

G *Every place I went, Hoovervilles – they were raided. . . .*
Guys with baseball bats, driving [everyone] out. . . .
  They were the Main Streeters. They were doing all right.
Merchants, storekeepers, landowners. They had [an attitude]
that was just awful to live with.

Ed Paulsen

H *Even the people that were quite well-to-do, they was*
ashamed. 'Cause they was eatin', and other people wasn't.

Mary Owsley

1 Look at extracts **A** and **B**. Mellon and Hoover had similar methods of calming people's fears. What were these methods?

2 Compare extracts **B** and **C**.
   a) How was Hoover's attitude changing?
   b) What is the first sign that Hoover was afraid of unrest or divisions in society?

3 Look at extracts **C**–**H**. What divisions do they reveal?

4 In extracts **D**, **E** and **F**, what feelings caused each person to speak or act as he did?

5 a) How does Rogers' statement remind us of Raskob's overconfidence?
   b) Which word shows that Rogers was thinking about corporations as well as wealthy individuals?
   c) Why do you think he fails to mention the overspending on shares and goods by ordinary citizens?

6 How would Mary Owsley have explained the raids on the Hoovervilles?

HOOVER AND THE BONUS ARMY

Self help

Throughout the early 1930s conditions in the United States got worse as more and more people lost their jobs. (The number passed 11 000 000 in 1932.) Despite the suffering, Hoover was still opposed to government 'interference'. He was not being lazy; perhaps he lacked imagination, but the main reasons for his inaction were his belief in 'rugged independence', and his dislike of the type of state control that existed in many countries such as the Soviet Union. Ideally, individuals should help themselves. The next best thing, in Hoover's view, was for companies, communities and other groups to help their own members. They should also find ways to restore prosperity. The governors of the separate states could help the needy if this was absolutely necessary; Hoover felt that anything was preferable to action by the central government. Here are some of the things he said to explain his beliefs:

> [I want to see] the free rise of ability, character and intelligence.

> Each industry should assist its own employees.

> Economic wounds must be healed by . . . the producers and consumers themselves.

> Each community and each State should assume its full responsibility for organization of employment and relief of distress.
> Quoted in W. laFeber and R. Polenberg's book
The American Century, 1979

Hoover's fears of government interference often seemed excessive. For example, he refused to reopen a disused hydroelectric power station which could generate electricity cheaply. Power plants were run by corporations; Hoover said that if the government ran one itself it would undermine the ideals of the nation.

Reluctant steps

As the Depression got worse and worse Hoover's government did take a few half-hearted steps. For example, he asked corporation bosses to keep their wage and production levels as high as possible. In one way this was a wise idea, for it might have slowed the cycle which was taking the country deeper and deeper into depression. However, things were already too bad for this to work. In fact, with profits getting smaller and smaller, most employers cut production and this meant reducing workers' pay – or taking away their jobs.

Hoover responded by cutting taxes. This meant that those who still had jobs could spend more money in the shops. It also meant that those who invested their money in business could keep a bigger share of the profits. Hoover thought that this would encourage more investment and thus bring about a business revival. However, the main effect of the cuts was to make the poorest people resentful. They felt that this was no time to favour the rich. They also resented the setting-up of a body called the Reconstruction Finance Corporation, which loaned enormous sums of money to banks, railways, insurance companies and other concerns which needed help. Some people called this 'millionaires' dole'; and they pointed out that the poor were often left to go hungry.

Another of Hoover's steps was to make the tariffs on imports higher than ever. This was one of his worst mistakes, for overseas countries responded by doing the same thing themselves. The rises caused a slump in international trade, and this helped to spread the Depression worldwide.

So that the countries of Western Europe could afford to buy more American goods, Hoover's government allowed them to put off paying the war-debts they owed. However, the Depression was so severe that this did little to help. The biggest effect of Hoover's move was to break the habit of paying the debts; as a result, the payments were never made again.

Lastly, in order to give people work, Hoover stepped up the building of things like dams and roads. This did provide jobs, but not nearly enough.

Feeding the poor

In the past, charities, councils and state authorities had sometimes been able to help the poor. However, as the number of needy people shot upwards, they were increasingly unable to cope:

destitute: homeless and penniless

> Only families that had become destitute, that had spent every dime of savings and sold every possession of value, could ordinarily qualify for assistance. Even then, those lucky enough to get on the relief rolls received barely enough for food. Rent, clothing, medical care – all these were considered luxuries.
>
> W. laFeber and R. Polenberg: The American Century, 1979

In September 1931, with 7 000 000 people out of work, Hoover set up the President's Organisation on Unemployment Relief. Led by a corporation chief called Walter Gifford, its task was to see that the poor were fed without the use of government money; instead it supported the failing efforts of charities, councils and state authorities. The organisation was also designed to reassure people that all was well, and Gifford tried very hard to do this. He denied that the poor were being neglected, and as Christmas approached he stated: 'There is every indication that each state will take care of its own this approaching winter.' However, Gifford later admitted in an interview that he did not know how many people were unemployed, how many were being helped already, or how much money was available in each state.

In the summer of 1932 Hoover finally started to give the states money to help with relief, but he gave them loans, not grants, and these were too small to prevent appalling suffering. In Chicago 'families [were] separated, husbands being sent to the men's shelter and wives to the women's shelter'. In another city, 'applications [for help were] not taken from unemployed Mexican or coloured families'. And in some towns children were weighed at the soup kitchens: the thin ones were fed; the rest had to wait until they too began to show signs of starvation.

Increasing unrest

During the Depression there were various outbreaks of anger and protest. In the following passage Ed Paulsen remembers events in San Francisco:

There'd be thousands of men.... They'd say 'OK, we're going to City Hall.'

I remember the demands: we demand work, we demand shelter for our families, we demand groceries, this kind of thing.... But you just knew society wasn't yielding. There was nothing coming....

There used to be cops on horseback in those days. There'd be some fighting. Finally it got to killing. I think they killed three people there that day, besides the wounded. It really got rough because the guys had brought a bunch of marbles and threw them on the street, and the horses were slipping and sliding around. This made the cops mad and they got rough.

Somehow you never expected to win. We had a built-in losing complex.... We were a gentle crowd. These were fathers, eighty per cent of them. They had held jobs and didn't want to kick society to pieces. They just wanted to go to work and they just couldn't understand.... We weren't talking revolution; we were talking jobs.

Quoted in Studs Terkel's book *Hard Times*, 1970

Questions

1 a) Who started the violence in San Francisco?
   b) Who did the killing?
   c) How clear is Paulsen on these two points?
   d) In what ways does he seem to be vague or unreliable?

2   Compare Hoover's aims with those of the men in San Francisco. How well do they match? How do they differ?

3   What was Hoover's probable view of what occurred and what it meant?

The Bonus Army

The Depression's most famous protest was staged by thousands of men who had fought in World War I. In 1924, the American government promised them a bonus of several hundred dollars each, to be paid in 1945.

During the Depression, many of these ex-servicemen began to demand their bonus at once. They had already risked their lives for their country; why should they risk starvation now instead of being promptly paid for what they had done? Their campaign reached its height in 1932, when a 'Bonus Army' of 22 000 angry men set out from homes (and Hoovervilles) all over America. Their destination was Washington, the American capital. Here they would set up a Hooverville to embarrass the government; they were also prepared to demonstrate in various ways to make their point.

Most of the men were penniless, so during the journey (which in many cases lasted several weeks) they had to beg for food and lifts. However, they found that many Americans wanted to help them. In the following passage Jim Sheridan, a member of the Bonus Army, tells what the journey was like for him:

We went down to the railyard and grabbed a freight train. Our first stop was in Peru, Indiana. We jungled up there for a little while, and then we bummed the town, so to speak. Go to different grocers and give them a tale of woe. They'd give us sausage or bread or

The Bonus Marchers setting up their Hooverville (called Bonus City)

meat or canned goods. Then we'd go back to the railroad yards, the jungle, where we'd ... sit around [a] fire and eat....

boxcars: freight containers

We'd generally be told by the [guards] when the train was ready to go. Some of these fellas had come with their families. Can you imagine women and children riding [in] boxcars? ... The [guards] ... would put two or three empty boxcars in the train so the bonus marchers could crawl into them and ride comfortable into Washington. Even the railroad detectives were very generous. Sometimes there'd be 50, 60 people ... sprawled out on the floor. [No] toilet – you had to hold it ... [for] 100 miles!

I remember ... we had to go through these mountain countries. The smoke from ... the engines, and the soot, would be flying back through the tunnels and coming into the boxcars.

Quoted in S. Terkel's book *Hard Times*, 1970

During the journey, Sheridan heard a woman scream in one of the tunnels. Later he found out that her baby had died of suffocation.

There were several other tragedies, but most of the adults reached Washington safely. By June the protesters' shanty town had been set up on the outskirts of Washington. As well as the 22 000 men, there were women and children. Some estimates put the total at nearly 40 000.

The government began to get worried. Until now the Depression had had less effect in the capital city than anywhere else. Officials in government offices should have known all about the nation's problems. However, they all had well-paid jobs, so the city was still quite prosperous. This meant that people were ignorant of what was going on elsewhere. The ragged state of some of the men in the Bonus Army came as a shock. In spite of this, the President said that the nation could not afford to pay them straight away. His officials called the protesters a 'rabble', but this was unfair since they organised their Hooverville like a military camp, with wartime strictness and discipline. Most daily papers were on the men's side. One called the protest 'a supreme escape gesture ... a flight from reality, a flight from hunger, from the cries of the starving ... from the harsh refusals of prospective employers'.

Questions

1   Look at the extract which begins on page 50.
    a)   What do you think the words 'jungled' and 'bummed' mean?
    b)   What is the main point the writer makes
       i)   about people's attitudes towards the Bonus Army;
       ii)   about the journey?

2   Look at the extract from the newspaper report.
    Do you think the writer was completely sympathetic with the Bonus Army? What does his attitude seem to be?

Bonus Marchers in the centre of respectable Washington

Persuasion and force

During July the government's nervousness increased, and protesters were offered loans to help them return to their homes. Many did not have homes to return to, but 5 000 people accepted the offer. The rest did as much as they could to increase the government's fear and embarrassment. For example, they marched in silence near official buildings, as if conducting funerals for Hoover and those who were on his side.

In the end, officials said that the men were led by Communists. The use of this label somehow made it easier for Hoover and others to ignore the men's claim. They also felt that the time had come for the army to drive them out of Washington.

Using the evidence: the Battle of Pennsylvania Avenue

The following reports differ greatly about the amount of violence that was used against the Bonus Army. They also describe different feelings afterwards:

MacArthur: an American general

A *[On 28 July] the great MacArthur came [riding] down Pennsylvania Avenue. Behind him were tanks, troops of the regular army.*

When these ex-soldiers wouldn't move they'd poke them with their bayonets and hit them on the head with the butt of a rifle. . . .

Driving the marchers out of the city

deplored: greatly regretted

A big coloured [man], about six feet tall, had a big American flag he was carrying. He was one of the bonus marchers. He turned and said, 'Don't try to push me. I fought for this flag. I fought for this flag in France and I'm gonna fight for it here on Pennsylvania Avenue.' The soldier hit him on the side of the legs with the bayonet. I think he was injured but I don't know if he was sent to hospital.

. . . The soldiers threw tear gas at them and vomiting gas. . . . They were younger than the marchers. It was like sons attacking their fathers. The next day the newspapers deplored the fact and so forth, but they realised the necessity of getting these men off. Because they were causing a health hazard to the city. MacArthur was looked upon as a hero.

Jim Sheridan, quoted in S. Terkel's book
Hard Times, 1970

B *When the [troops] came out, what else could they do? They just walked off. . . .*

I remember when they came back from Washington. . . . They had a sort of reunion. It was nice weather, summertime. And all kinds of people came to visit 'em. They had a flag spread out, and everyone was throwin' money in . . . showin' that they were welcomin' 'em back and were all for 'em. They had quite a time. After that, where they went, nobody knows.

E. Schalk, quoted in S. Terkel's book *Hard Times*, 1970

HERE·LIES
WILLIAM·HUSHKA
WORLD·WAR·VETERAN
KILLED
IN · THE · BATTLE
AGAINST·STARVATION
AT·WASHINGTON·D.C.
JULY · 28TH · 1932
BY·ORDER·OF
HERBERT·HOOVER

Opposite: *a cartoon tribute to someone who died when the Bonus Marchers were driven out of Washington*

1 Look again at passages **A** and **B**, which contain reports by people who witnessed events in July 1932. Which witness was in the Bonus Army? How might this have affected his attitude?

2 Witness **A** says he doesn't know whether the black protester was sent to hospital. Why do you think he makes this remark?

3 The witnesses disagree about how much violence was used. Which witness does the photograph on page 53 tend to support? What dangers do you think there are in trusting a single photograph?

4 How much violence do *you* think was used? Be sure to consider all the evidence, and try to say how you reached your conclusions.

5 a) Why do you think witness **A** calls the general 'the *great* MacArthur'?
   b) Why does he call the protesters 'ex-soldiers', rather than using some other word?

6 The witnesses say that the protesters and their supporters had flags. Why did they want them?

7 Look at the end of passage **A** and think about conditions elsewhere in America. How fair do you think the newspapers were?

8 How does witness **A** try to gain your sympathy in his final paragraph? How might Hoover have answered the points he made?

From protest to hope

After the defeat of the Bonus Army there was one more major protest by those who were suffering hardship. This began in August 1932, when struggling farmers refused to send their produce to market. The idea of this was to force prices up and create a national shortage of food. They hoped that Hoover's government would then guarantee higher prices in future. However, the farmers' plan was a failure, partly because many thousands of farmers insisted on getting their produce to market, even though the prices were low. They were deeply in debt and felt they should get what money they could.

By the end of September the farmers' protest had come to an end. The Depression was getting worse and worse, but most Americans now began to pin their hopes on the autumn presidential elections. Hoover's chances of being voted in for a second term of office seemed extremely small; his Democratic opponent Franklin Roosevelt believed in a far more active form of government. He was offering voters a 'New Deal' and there seemed little doubt that they would accept it.

INDEX

Numerals in **bold** denote illustrations